S. O. S.

Survival Guide for Teachers, Old and New

Greta Woolley, M.Ed.

Contents

Foreword . . . vii
by Aimee Ballans

Preface . . . xv
Invitation To Move . . . xix

1. Why Me? Why You? Why Now? . . . 1
2. Faith Stories . . . 11
3. Life Plans . . . 21
4. Balancing Your Account . . . 31
5. Harness Your Everyday Powers . . . 39
6. Spaces and Places . . . 47
7. Road to Resilience . . . 57
8. I'm So Glad We Had This Time Together . . . 65

Afterword . . . 69
Acknowledgments . . . 73
About the Author . . . 75

Copyright © 2023 Greta Woolley

All rights reserved. No parts of this book may be reproduced or used in any manner without the prior written permission of the copyright owner, except for the use of brief quotations in a book review.

Paperback: 979-8-9889757-0-0

Ebook: 979-8-9889757-1-7

First paperback edition September 2023

Breakthrough Books

*To my parents, my first and best teachers.
The ones who taught me about the power of words.
I will love you until all the days have turned to hours, and all the
hours have turned to minutes, and all the minutes have turned to
seconds, and all the seconds in the universe have run out of time.
And that will be forever.*

Foreword
by Aimee Ballans

THE GREAT COMMISSION

I knew I wanted to be a teacher since the first "career day" in kindergarten, when I put on my mom's pencil skirt, a pair of glasses, and tied my long hair up in a bun to participate in our career parade. Over the ensuing years, I hardly wavered from this plan, even through my crazy teen years when being a teacher was a less-than-glamorous career choice. (I did briefly entertain being a meteorologist, but quickly tossed that to the side when I realized how much science was involved.)

I am a first-generation college-graduate. The youngest of three girls, my GED-earning parents were just happy we each were graduating with a high school diploma. But I had teachers who saw more in me and began helping me craft a vision for my life early on. If not for these teachers pulling back the curtain on how to fill out college applications and apply for student loans, I am not sure where I would be today.

I kept that gratitude close to my heart every day when I walked into my own classroom, knowing firsthand that education changes lives. And teachers who take the time to see the brilliance in their students and help knock barriers out of the way are often a huge factor in having access to that life-changing college educational experience.

For eight years, I was a high school social studies and AVID (Advancement Via Individual Determination) teacher. My first teaching job was at the high school I opened as a student and later graduated from. My last teaching job was at a high-needs school I opened as a teacher. AVID definitely taught me lessons about how to see the potential in all students, help remove barriers to opportunities, and empower students to thrive.

These became the lessons that I brought with me to my next role as a New Teacher Mentor. For six years, I had the chance to grow and develop the mentoring program for teachers new to the profession, and I absolutely fell in love with this work!

I clearly remember the day I had to tell my AVID kids that I was leaving the classroom. I had been with them two years and they were about to start their senior year. We were a family, and it was devastating to have to say good-bye on the cusp of their biggest year—a year when I knew they would need me the most to help them cross the finish line strong. As we sat in a circle facing each other, tears pouring down my face, they told me how much of a difference I had made in their lives. How no other teacher had ever cared so much for them. No other teacher had ever made them believe in themselves.

As I wiped my tears away, I knew I had made the right decision and told them that this was exactly the reason why I was taking this new job as a mentor. That a student should never get to 11th grade and say no teacher cared about them, tried to help them, or believed in them. I made a promise to my students that I would use my role as a mentor to help create teachers who loved their students, loved their jobs, and were the best at creating healthy teaching and learning conditions that enabled them to take care of students for their entire careers. I felt like my AVID kids were sending me out with a great commission to go forth and create a legion of teachers who would care for their students the way I cared for them, and to this day that is what I aim to do.

I now work for an education non-profit where I get to teach mentors and coaches how to mentor. I help school districts of every size and demographic create mentoring programs and/or develop coaches who are able to address the needs of their students and create optimal learning environments, while disrupting the inequities that steal opportunities from kids to thrive.

I help raise the conscious competence of developing mentors and experienced coaches to better understand themselves and their craft in order to pay forward to the teachers they support, so they in turn can pay it forward to each student in their classes. I help to humanize the teaching and learning process by slowing down teachers, mentors, and coaches. I give them the permission, knowledge, and skills to see those they work with as individual *people* and consider how to pour into each of them so their brilliance can bubble to the surface.

DIGGING DEEP

I spend a lot of time in schools across the country, and teachers have been hit hard by life over the last few years. It wasn't only the pandemic, but I do think the pandemic had a huge impact on the social-emotional well-being of educators.

For the veteran educators, we dug DEEP and made it through for our kids, but when we got to the other side there was no rest. No opportunity to regroup and replenish. Just the urgency to "get back to work" and start filling in the gaps! Educators were exhausted and have been exhausted ever since. They are working with students who have some of the greatest needs we have seen in years (academic and social-emotional) with little-to-no guidance on how to help them. We are all building the ship as we are sailing these post-pandemic waters. Layer on the political and social climate of the last eight years, where teachers as humans are questioned for our motivation, lifestyle, and intentions.

Yikes! It's hard for us to hold each other up because we have all been in it together, but what Greta offers in this book is acknowledgement and understanding, along with the perspective that life is filled with peaks and valleys, and we all have the power in us to grow through these challenges.

She tells us not to ignore the struggle, but that the struggle is shaping us if we give ourselves the time and space to understand it. She reminds us that we need to give ourselves the grace and care to heal, and that we do not have to do it alone. This is such an important message for our new teachers. They may not have been on the front lines of the last few years, but they are walking into what must feel like a post-apocalyptic world. The veterans may not be able to give them the same support, hope, and encouragement as in years past. But we are all still here. And our strength comes from seeing that humanity in each other, taking a moment to check-in, and cheering each other on.

The important lessons in this book address intangible emotional intelligence that is needed for a teacher to thrive. Teacher-prep programs and/or alternative certification programs are often hyper-focused on getting teachers up to speed with the content they will be teaching (which is important). But we all know that teaching is so much more than content plans. This book pulls back the curtain on the Social and Emotional Learning (SEL) teachers need to cultivate within ourselves to not just be successful, but to thrive and enjoy the amazing job we get to do.

MODELING THE MODEL

This book is modeling the model in its design. Greta put this book together with care and intention to humanize the reading experience by continually inviting the reader to turn inside, think deeply about who they are and their story, and consider how that is showing up in their practice. By inviting us to slow down a little, reflect on our own emotions and responses (which are not only okay, but needed to heal and thrive), and engage in real (and realistic) self-care, this book turns the reading experience into an interactive invitation for growth. In these pages, you will find so many practical steps and exercises to not only do yourself, but also do for the teachers you coach and/or students you teach.

GO WHERE YOU ARE READY TO GO

This is such a delightful read in so many ways. It felt like a conversation with my own mentor—someone who has been where I have been, who is not afraid of real talk (which is so important to anyone who has really been in the trenches), and who has the real-world experience to offer sage wisdom.

Also appealing: this book does not promise "10 Steps to Fix All Your Problems." There is an honesty woven into the fabric of this book from the beginning that there is no easy fix or magic wand. Instead, in true mentor fashion, Greta invites us to consider meaningful questions so we can get what we need and go where we are ready to go. In these pages, I love that new teachers are hearing a counter-narrative to the veterans who are worn-down and defeated.

Greta is a teaching veteran who has stood the test of time and continues to reflect, grow, and reinvent herself—which is what we all need to do to thrive (and a theme that you will see throughout this book). For the veterans, it offers a reminder that we have been through so much and are capable of so much more, but that does not happen by accident. We do not passively thrive; we thrive because of choices we make that are grounded in knowing our "why."

I also love that this is a quick read. I read this whole book in about two hours, which is about how much spare time a busy teacher has. I was engaged with the personal stories, and loved the choose-my-own-adventure lists as springboards to decide how I wanted to use the wisdom being offered. I plan to go back and reread chapters, as needed, and take away different nuggets, depending on the options and exercises I choose to explore.

HOPE AND UNDERSTANDING

Greta leaves us with hope and understanding that our experiences are shaping us and preparing us for the next part of our story. There is a uniquely special feeling when you get to be in space with Greta. A vibrant loving energy pours off her. You can feel her energy when you read this book. I am so lucky and blessed that I have been able to experience Greta in real life; I have seen the positive effect her energy has on the teachers and kids she works with every day, or just happens to pass in the hall.

Many readers may never get to meet her in person, but as I read the words on each page, I hear her voice and am enveloped in that same energy, that same love, that I feel when I am with her. I hope, dear reader, you realize what a gift this is. I hope the love you feel as you read this beautiful book helps to nourish your soul in a way that allows you to share that love with others.

— AIMEE BALLANS
Director of Programs and Partnerships
New Teacher Center
July 2023

Preface

There is a destiny which makes us brothers; none goes his way alone. All that we send into the lives of others comes back into our own.

— Edwin Markham

During my entire childhood, a picture hung in our home. It was painted by one of my mother's best friends who was an incredibly beautiful, intellectual, and insanely talented artist. For the background, her hands had skillfully merged shades of burnt orange, yellow, brown, and beige. Layered upon that, she had block-printed the above quote from Markham: "There is a destiny which makes us brothers; none goes his way alone. All that we send into the lives of others comes back into our own." The words repeated over and over, until at last the canvas was void of empty space.

I would often stare at the words, wondering what they meant, most curious about the artist's decision to use such striking repetition. Little me had absolutely no idea what the answer was to either of those questions. *Weird words and lots of them,* I must have thought in my five-year-old mind.

Zoom forward five decades later, to the woman I have become today. The one who looks back in awe at the sheer masterpiece that unknowingly guided me. I get it. I get it now. There is a connection between all of us. We need each other. When we pay attention, we will notice invisible strings that pull us toward one another. When we are brave enough to extend our hands in times of need, there will unquestionably be another hand waiting to hold ours, ready to pull us forward if we are prepared to move. A sister or a brother, who has seemingly been anticipating our unveiling, standing strong and tall and ready to assure us that we are in this life together. When we learn to give with unconditional love from our hearts, we open ourselves up to receiving from other beating hearts that same magnified love.

This, dear reader, is the purpose of this book. My dream is that this book becomes a guide for self-reflection and life illustration that will aid you in your journey. Continuing the never-ending cycle of sending love into the world guarantees it will return to us tenfold.

I have been an educator for 35 wonderful years. Throughout my career and my life, I have experienced tremendous joy, along with heartbreaking agony. I've seen a thing or two—and I suspect you have as well. What I have personally learned in my own life is that immense power comes from reflection and storytelling. After decades of intense contemplation and a deep desire for understanding and growth, I have been able to use my own narrative to restore from within. For a long time, I searched for external bandages to heal the hurting parts. It was not until I began to share my stories, and search for healing from the inside-out, that the real evolution unfolded.

My life has been full of abundant happiness, a highly functional family, joy, education, love, and more. I say this because I know that every story does not include these privileges. I say it because I must make it *crystal* clear that no book is able to help someone who is not in a safe place, ready, and armed to do the hard work that comes with self-examination. I have picked up a thousand books that I could not read until I was truly ready to receive the gifts that patiently awaited me with every turn of a page.

This book is written for professional teachers and educators. However, I believe the title of "teacher" fits most of us. Everybody is a teacher in some capacity. Mothers, fathers, business owners, pastors, authors, lawyers, doctors, therapists, mechanics, hairdressers, cashiers, servers...

We are all teachers **and** students. Why not let our greatest lessons pour from our very souls? Each chapter of this book was designed to illuminate part of my self-work and life lessons, followed by a guided reflection that you can explore to enhance your own story-telling and personal growth.

I began this book because in my work with teachers, I found a crisis exploding all around me. We are wounded and crawling. Bleeding and bandaged. Dehydrated and desperate. We are searching for excellence in our profession, while craving the balanced and beautiful lives we so richly deserve.

While I am honest about the pain that I witness among both experienced educators and struggling beginning teachers, this book is a haven for hope and optimism. I invite you to join me in my belief that our profession is the most noble and worthy of all. We are blessed with a gift that out-measures all other careers: one of potent belonging and connectedness with the entire world. It is our profession that begets all others. In a world full of disconnected adults and children searching for strength and unity, may this book be a large dose of what you need to believe that you are valued, worthy, loved, noticed, and integral to this planet. May it be shouted from the highest mountaintop: schools are the places where our greatest sense of belonging is nurtured into full bloom.

When beginning this book, my first instinct was to "save." *Save* our teachers. But you'll see—I'm smarter than that. You don't need to be saved. You already have what you need inside of you.

So, start reading if you're ready to "receive." The good news is that it doesn't require superpowers. In fact, quite the opposite is true: we must kindle our "everyday" powers.

Take my hand. You don't need to do this alone. I promise you, just as Edwin Markham said, there is a destiny that made us brothers and sisters. All that you send into this work from your personal history will come back into your own life with new insights and greater power for a brighter future.

Invitation To Move

The world is full of magical things patiently waiting for our wits to grow sharper.

— Bertrand Russell

You don't need to be an educator to be fully aware that the state of our schools is nothing short of desperate. Teachers are dropping like flies, experiencing lack of sleep, feelings of overwhelm, poor health, stress, anxiety, depression, withdrawal and so much more. This list is too long and too full of all the wrong words to describe these superhumans who have devoted their lives to bettering the lives of others. They are crawling toward the door marked EXIT, unsure where to turn for help. Colleagues are bolting to become corporate trainers or project managers or, more likely, supplementing their teacher salaries as part-time

Uber drivers and babysitters making ten- to fifteen-dollars-an-hour just to barely survive in this economy.

We must create a movement of great energy and power to reinstate the magic show. Educators deserve the "oooohs and ahhhhs" that should follow their acts of refreshing the consciousness of the world in which we live. These humans who take teaching seriously do not merely sit flipping through pre-made lesson plans, so that children might be on "page 43" of some random curriculum by Thanksgiving. Rather, they perfect the art of raising awareness about our world, giving meaning to words and numbers, choreographing steps in the dance of life.

Teachers deserve attention. This is their *calling*—helping students increase their awareness of the world; collect ideas and impressions; avoid a lack of engagement in high-quality learning experiences—and yet many of them are left alone, feeling they have dialed the wrong number.

Carl Rogers stated, "How does it happen that the deeper we go into ourselves as particular and unique, seeking our own individual identity, the more we find the whole human species?" Not one of us, whether we are teachers or students (and guess what? We are ***always*** both!) can continue to exist without each other. In order to change and grow, we need the leadership of our amazing guides: our teachers, professors, mentors, gurus.

Our educators aid us in transcending life's conditions and awaken us to the sense of brotherhood that can and should exist within all mankind, helping us to confirm and affirm our existence.

This book is an invitation to pause and slow down. Often, we must slow down to go fast! In kindergarten, our students shouldn't be expected to become advanced readers by the first month of school, and by fifth grade we don't have to be finished with all of "life's lessons." Treating five-year-olds like second-graders and fifth-graders like adults does not align with the human brain.

Should teachers be expected to demonstrate excellence in the areas of content and pedagogy? YES! Relationships? YES! Knowledge of students? YES! Lesson planning? You bet! Assessment? Agreed...but let's truly realize that our capacity and impact as teachers reaches far beyond standardized testing that requires even preschoolers, who are in a constant state of development, to perform in one moment in time.

What our teachers **shouldn't** have to do is become experts in mental health services for their own anxiety, depression, fear, and uncertainty. They **shouldn't** be holding multiple jobs, struggling to figure out how to send their own kids to college, or dreaming of the day when they turn seventy and can finally re-do the kitchen!

Yes, I dream of the house make-over, but it's really about so much more than that. Teachers consistently deplete themselves, to the point that their emotional bandwidth for their own families is compromised. At times in my own teaching journey, it has felt like I am tricking myself. I tell myself, "If not me, then who?" to validate overworking in the name of helping children. We must do this to keep running back to school. However, catching up on our own emotional regulation is a race we can't win.

I don't want to live in a world where educators become extinct and my grandchildren wander the earth inquiring,

"Where did all the teachers go?" So, I'm sending out an S.O.S: Save our Ship. In Morse code: "three dits, three dats, and another three dits." I proclaim our vessel in distress needs some of "this," some of "that," and a little bit more of "this." In other words: self-empowerment, emotional support, and life plans that include personal and professional needs.

We are in danger, and we need help immediately. The first step is equipping yourself to move. It is *you* who must desire to save yourself.

Keep reading. That's how we'll start.

A movement begins with one voice calling out to others to join the chorus.

Chapter 1

Why Me? Why You? Why Now?

Nothing, I suspect, is more astonishing in any man's life than the discovery that there do exist people, very like himself.
-C.S. Lewis

My Teacher Story

From the time I was a little girl, I was teaching and mothering a plethora of dolls ranging from Barbie size to the bigger-than-life Raggedy Ann doll that was taller than me when I first met her one Christmas morning at the age of four. I say with humor that I should have seen my early tendencies for codependency. I felt guilty for getting to sleep in the bed every night, so I started camping out on the floor and "tucking her in," so she could get a good night's rest.

I was born a caretaker and a teacher. Each day and each night was consumed by lining up at least twenty dolls, every single one of them with a name and distinct personality, all open to my early talents for differentiating instruction!

My father began as a Methodist minister, but quickly moved into the field of education, where he found himself serving a larger congregation of people longing for strong, loving, and meaningful relationships and contribution. He held important positions such as the Supervisor of Language Arts for the parish in which I resided in Baton Rouge, Louisiana. He later traveled the entire country as a vice president for a company that supported juvenile delinquents and adjudicated delinquents. My mother wasn't just a stay-at-home mom who had dinner on the table every night at 5pm. She was a homemaker and everything that she did inside of our home enabled my father to provide for us through his actions outside of our house. As a family, we perfected a model of support delivery to all the "underdogs" of the world, and we did it with pride.

Both of my parents loved the arts and self-reflection, so I was raised with a true appreciation of music, performance, and good conversation revolving around many deep topics about the meaning of life and our place in it. There was always laughter, learning, family, and friends and many, many, many pots of coffee brewing. My sister, brother, and I all did well in school and got through with very few bumps in the educational pathway. We did not have much from a material point of view, but life always felt "rich." So, when I turned eighteen and graduated from high school, I found myself driving to the University of Florida, ready to continue the work of being Raggedy Ann's mother and first teacher. In fact, she sat in the passenger seat, all belted up as I literally cried the entire drive to Gainesville, Florida.

I was crying because I was excited. Crying because I was ready to begin adulting. Crying because I wanted this. Crying because I was full of apprehension, with no real idea about what I wanted to be when I grew up. As the year passed, and I found myself having to declare a major, my heart vacillated between actress, psychologist, and teacher. What could be a better fit than a special education teacher? I could perform every day. Provide instruction and therapy. Root for the underdog. Continue my own hunger for learning. *Okay, let's go.* And so I did. It began. This is my teacher story.

However, what I don't think I realized when I first constructed this story were all the details of my life that were still left out. The circumstances that I would dive into after the sudden death of my brother in a head-on collision with a semi-truck two weeks before my college graduation. The thirteen years that I would help my mother and sister to care for my father with early-onset Alzheimer's. Or the seven years after that, where I became my mother's arms and legs, carrying her through a fierce journey of grief and her own passing.

I would come to live out the details of my life that contributed to every part of who I am and why I was truly called to be an educator. A caretaker. A believer. An encourager. A communicator. A trainer. A mentor. An understander of human behavior. The details unraveled like a thread being pulled from the hem of a ragged dress that just kept getting longer and longer. We'll save those for the chapters on faith stories and resilience. But I can end with this:

I am a teacher. I was born to be a teacher. I will always be a teacher. I was meant to be a teacher. I will live, breathe, and die being a teacher. I am proud to be a teacher. I will always elevate, support, and cry out for other teachers. I will fight to save our teachers. I will never give up on teachers. I believe that teachers are the most important humans on the planet.

I am a teacher. I was born to be a teacher. I will always be a teacher. I was meant to be a teacher. I will live, breathe, and die being a teacher. I am proud to be a teacher. I will always elevate, support, and cry out for other teachers. I will fight to save our teachers. I will never give up on teachers. I believe that teachers are the most important humans on the planet.

∽

What is Your Teacher Story?

- Take a moment to reflect upon your teacher story.
- Let a stream of consciousness flow over you as you find your words without over-thinking.
- Now, go back and ask yourself: could there be other factors that contributed to your decision-making? How does it feel to consider those impacting forces? Are you proud? Emotional? Content? etc.
- Imagine the positive impact of declaring your teacher story. In what ways could this connect you

to your origin and lead you to new destinations? List ways it might keep you strong during a challenge, or inspire you to pull deeper from your source when you are feeling motivated to do even "bigger" things.
- Having trouble deciding how your story should be told? Think back to teachers who impacted you (good and "bad"); create a timeline of your life and look for defining moments.

Why Now?

- Ask yourself: Why am I reading this book now?
- What do I want to accomplish through this journey for myself, my students and my family and friends?
- What may be holding me back from becoming the best and healthiest version of myself?
- What does my self-talk sound like? Am I being kind and understanding? Do I go down roads of self-judgment and insecurity? How can I create scripts that serve me in the best way possible, so that I might care for myself and others productively?

Take-Away Time

- We all have a story. Our stories are not all the same, but inevitably we will find the similarities that bind us together in this extremely difficult but rewarding field of education. Perhaps the Wiz said it best in *The Wizard of Oz* when he told Dorothy, "It ain't

enough to know where you're going; you gotta know where you're coming from." We all must create a personal baseline from which we can vary, but to which we can always return.
- Don't worry if you cannot immediately construct a "best-seller" for your story. As you continue to read, you will see that the value of my story revealed itself after years of self-reflection and my search for meaning in my life as I got older. In turn, my teacher story became a launching pad for personal growth.
- There is always "more to the story." Continue to study yourself and look for the hidden details, as they will help guide your transformation and evolution.

Mindful Moment

- Write a letter to the universe thanking her for this moment in time. There is no right or wrong way. Just show up to the paper and start writing. You have a story to tell that other people want to hear. Give thanks for all the moments that have built your foundation for your "right now."
- Use poetry or prose to write about what an epic teacher you are! I wrote these two poems when I was an instructional mentor wearing many different hats.

I Am, IM

*I am an Instructional Mentor-**IM**!*
*I am an **IM**agineer with **IM**easurable ideas for turning what may feel **IM**possible at times into reality.*
I pull from my own inspiration so that
*I can in turn "**IM**"spire others to find their best selves.*
*The work that I do is **IM**portant because*
*all roads lead back to children and the **IM**mense job that we have as educators to prepare them for life in the most **IM**pactful way possible.*
*I do not seek to create more **IM**ages of myself.*
Quite the opposite.
*I humbly bare my own **IM**perfections so that others might break down **IM**penetrable walls that may prevent the kind of self-reflection that makes the "**IM**movable" movable.*
*I will not **IM**pede the growth of my sisters and brothers by pushing my own agenda.*
*Instead, I will take very seriously the **IM**plications of my work and choose the **IM**mediate response of active listening over the **IM**pulsivity of **IM**printing my own ideas on*

> top of the newborn ideas of beginning
> teachers and experienced colleagues.
> I don't mean to **IM**ply that I don't have BIG
> ideas of my own, but I challenge myself to
> listen carefully to the BIG ideas of others as
> they are equally **IM**pressive.

Who am I?
I am an instructional Mentor-**IM**!

∼

Who Am I?

IM...
An Instructional Mentor-IM!
I support everything from Headstart babies to
*   eighth-grade band.*
I celebrate the diversity that greets me
as I travel to the bookends of my district and
*   everywhere in between.*
There are no boundaries I won't cross, no school
*   doors I won't walk through*
if they lead me to love and learning.
Who Am I?
IM...
A highly passionate gardener
who believes in empowering others
through the cultivation of professional inquiry
and ambitious expectations for learning.

Who Am I?
IM...
A hungry giant seeking opportunities for professional growth;
a floating fairy scoping out healthy margins for myself and my people;
a dancer in communities of learning, gracefully bending
with the flexibility and responsiveness
of a prima ballerina to the music that is playing.
Who Am I?
IM...
A detective searching for entry points,
a library shelf full of books that enhance knowledge and practice,
a lawyer stating her case through countless artifacts of evidence,
a record-keeper who reflects on ideas
so that I might build upon my strengths to expand upon my seedlings.
Who Am I?
IM...
A model of respect, honesty, and integrity
willing to both give and accept feedback so that I promote growth.
I am an Instructional Mentor...
IM!

Ritual Reinforcement

- Consider creating a daily ritual that will mindfully guide you into your teaching day. For example, re-reading an inspiring note from a student, parent, or colleague. Or maybe reading a poem or motivational words. I have read the same thing every day for the past 35 years, and I have it framed on my desk to remind me of the power that I harness each day as an educator. What will your daily ritual reading say?

Daily Ritual Reading

I have come to a frightening conclusion: I am the decisive element in the classroom. It is my personal approach that creates the climate. It is my daily mood that makes the weather. As an educator, I possess tremendous power to make a child's life miserable or joyous. I can be a tool of torture or an instrument of inspiration. I can humiliate or humor, hurt or heal. In all situations, it is my response that decides whether a crisis will be escalated or de-escalated, and a child humanized or de-humanized.

— Haim G. Ginott

Chapter 2

Faith Stories

To have faith is to trust yourself to the water. When you swim, you don't grab hold of the water, because if you do you will sink and drown. Instead, you relax, and float.

— Alan Wilson Watts

To Infinity and Beyond

I hadn't thought about it until I met with my personal writing coach, but perhaps this book is, indeed, a letter to myself. Something that has taken me 35 years to birth because it takes a long time to bring worthwhile things to full term.

And so, my teacher story begins to take on greater depth. If I could jump inside a time machine, I would take this letter directly back to the 23-year-old me who began her first year of teaching on the heels of an incredible tragedy that would change the way her life looked forever, and I would hug her and keep holding her even after she tried to let go. I would whisper in her ear, "You did good, kid. You did good." I would let warm tears run down my cheeks as I stroked her long, silky black hair, and when she began to shake from sobbing, I would rock her back and forth like I did my own newborn daughters, singing a sweet and soothing lullaby written only for her. The words would penetrate her soul and speak to her of things to come. They would guide her toward her helpers, already waiting to lead her safely through her journey. And in this embrace, I would begin to tell my former self about all the things she would be able to accomplish throughout her life because of this *one moment* in time.

As weird as this sounds, many amazing and beautiful and meaningful things transpired because of that trauma.

I still vividly remember that first second when I found out, as if it were just yesterday. I was studying for my last exam before I was set to graduate from the University of Florida. I had pulled an all-nighter writing a twenty-page paper after devouring two pots of coffee. *Boom. Only one more exam, and I am two weeks away from one of the happiest and biggest milestones of my life—becoming a college grad! Please, God. Let's make this happen.*

The phone rang, just like any other day. But when I answered it, the deep sound of an unfamiliar voice asked, "Is this Greta?"

"Yes, it is."

"This is Deputy Miller. How old are you, Greta?"

"Twenty-two," I said, wondering why in the world that even mattered.

"Then you must have been younger than your brother," he said.

What does that mean? I thought.

"There's been a terrible accident. Your brother was killed. You need to get home."

Later, I would learn that my parents were already frozen in such stifling grief that they couldn't even make the phone call to tell me what had happened.

Immediately, I hung up and stared into the oval-shaped mirror that hung above my phone. The young man I was dating at the time unexpectedly showed up, and I couldn't even speak for what felt like an eternity. He kept asking me, "What happened?" In return, I could only stare at him.

We eventually made the drive back to Tampa to find my mother pounding her fists upon my father's chest, demanding that he "bring Tony home." But Tony would never be home again, and neither would the woman who gave birth to me. That woman died the same day.

Splash! My introduction to grief began. In a slightly comatose state, I returned to school to complete my master's degree in education before graduating once more and heading back to Tampa as a beginning teacher. I made myself so busy that it would have been impossible to find room to acknowledge what had happened. I managed the Häagen-Dazs Ice-Cream shop until 2 a.m. each night. I wrote a thesis paper on teacher wait-time and intertrial interval duration with student questioning (in other words, the number of seconds you wait before getting the answer to the question). I was a teaching assistant for one of my professors. I was so tired that I could fall asleep standing up if the wall was kind enough to hold me that day.

The real pain didn't start until I moved closer to my mother and took my first job in a self-contained classroom for severely emotionally disturbed students grades four through six. Please don't think less of me if I say they were the craziest cats in town, but they were. And, maybe, just maybe—so was I.

I didn't know what I didn't know, and so I meandered my way through a thick, dark forest of new learning and emotional overload without once—and I mean once—realizing that I had no support to process the huge loss I had just experienced. I did not speak one word of this to another soul, and I will never understand why I didn't. At the time, it was just my "normal."

Most nights, my mother would call me after drinking half a bottle of scotch, and she would cry and scream about my brother's death. I would listen until about 4 a.m., lay back down for an hour of sleep, and then shower and head off for another workday. (Oh, by the way, 23-year-old me, that WAS NOT NORMAL. You didn't have to answer the phone every night.) My initiation into the world of superpowers began that year.

I remember one vivid weekend night when I was visiting my mother and she threw an envelope at me and proclaimed, "You need to see this!"

It turns out that I did *not* need to see it. Apparently, a photographer who thought we might want to sue the truck driver who hit my brother, had passed the scene of the accident and taken photos. He sent us several glossy prints of my brother's broken body on the side of the road. My brother, Tony, had been killed in a head-on collision with a semi-truck on his way to USF, where he was about to get his master's degree in education. He was thrown from the car and broke almost every single bone in his body. Those images still hide in the darkest corners of my mind.

Oh, for gracious sakes, Greta, where in the world are you going with this? You ready, Lil Greta? Thirty-five years later, this is what I want you to know:

- You will find more joy in life than you ever thought your heart could hold.
- Your mother will be reborn into an even better version of herself, and you will have years to heal beside her.
- You will be initiated into a "club" that—while perhaps you would prefer to not belong in—will allow you to have compassion and empathy for others who are grieving, in a way that moves mountains.
- You will begin to collect what you now refer to as your "faith" stories—the ones that validate that you can do hard things! That you believe and find value in all of life's stories. That the light is always waiting on the other side of your darkest nights.
- You have a gift for helping others get to the "other side" of doubt, fear, anxiety, uncertainty, etc.
- You will become an amazing teacher, coach, and

mentor, with many stories to tell, and great healing powers.

The last time I saw my brother was two months before he passed away. Our birthdays were two days apart. I had been home for the weekend, and as I was leaving to return to Gainesville, for some reason Tony yelled out to me, "Hey, Greta. What do you think infinity is?"

(I should add here that my big brother was muuuuuch smarter than me, having graduated with his B.A. degree as a double-major in physics and Russian. *Who does that?*)

"Infinity? I dunno. On and on and on," I think I must have said.

I wish I could answer now. Because I would tell him, "Infinity is my love for you. It has no beginning, and it knows no end. It blows through my faith stories like a breath of rainbow-colored warmth, reminding me that all the answers to all of life's questions are already inside of me, if I just wait and listen. Infinity is the time I have on my side to do and understand all things that are truly worth doing. Infinity is the time I am willing to wait if it means I get to see you once again."

Infinity is my love for you. It has no beginning, and it knows no end. It blows through my faith stories like a breath of rainbow-colored warmth, reminding me that all the answers to all of life's questions are already inside of me, if I just wait and listen. Infinity is the time that I have on my side to do and understand all things that are truly worth doing. Infinity is the time I am willing to wait if it means I get to see you once again.

What is one of your faith stories?

- We all have unique and beautiful stories to tell. Some are full of joy radiating from every line that is written or spoken, while others depict the very real nature of life that involves every human feeling, including great pain and sorrow. What we hopefully come to realize is that we must feel "all the feels" and that all our stories should be held on sacred ground for only those worthy enough to honor their truth. Your faith stories are the ones that come full-circle, playing themselves out from problem to solution, and encapsulate your ability to overcome challenges.

How does this impact the educator that you are now?

- In what ways can your collection of faith stories grow you as an educator?
- Knowing that you can and will continue to tackle confrontations and challenges as a teacher, how might your faith stories aid you in the process?

Take-Away Time

- We all have what I like to call "faith stories." The ones that build our character, that grow us in immeasurable ways, that connect us to the human experience, and that prove to us that we have what it takes to overcome any difficulties that come our way. It should be noted that some of these obstacles will require tremendous back-up from others who support us.
- Imagine going back and talking to your former self—the one standing in that very first moment of profound grief, adversity or pain. We all must stand in that crucible at one time or another. Guide your present mind into a place that allows for no judgment. No shame. No timelines. Listen to your wisdom as it whispers, "I am doing the best I can, right now. I can handle this. I am protected by a force of love that guides and watches over me. I may not understand this right now, but my strength will come."

Mindful Moment

- Find a quiet space to imagine something difficult or challenging that you have faced. Imagine what it would look like for that situation to be peaceful, healed, or new again. Envision yourself playing out the most successful outcome possible. This doesn't mean that you are taking away the "hard" part, it just means that you are allowing yourself to trust the water to support you. Relax and float.

Ritual Reinforcement

- What daily rituals could you create to honor your faith stories? Perhaps you can chant a specific mantra related to your experience. For example: "I can handle this! I have done hard things in the past, and I can do them again." Or maybe: "I may not feel it right now, but light is waiting on the other side of this."

Daily Ritual Reading

- Make a list of go-to gurus. My current crush is on Brené Brown. If I could choose any next-door neighbor, it would be her. Oh, boy! I could only imagine the faith stories we could share! Her written works include multiple passages that are rich with inspiration. Dr. Becky Bailey, I would love to have a cup of coffee and a cookie with you as well, please. Reading this expert's work has guided me through many joyful and challenging days at work.

Chapter 3

Life Plans

3 Dits, 3 Dats, and Another 3 Dits!

You save yourself, or you remain unsaved.

— Alice Sebold

As trite as it may sound, I have always loved the saying: "Failing to plan is planning to fail." Nobody knows for sure if good ol' Ben Franklin stated this in 1790, but I'm giving him full cred. Regardless, *whoever* said it was on to something, and most educators today will agree wholeheartedly on the importance of good planning.

However, good planning involves more savvy than one might think.

Well-prepared educators are undoubtedly competent in their understanding of objectives and standards, necessary materials, background knowledge of students, modes of learning and instruction, procedures and management of student conduct, and assessment (along with the 5,000 other decisions they may be making in one hour)...

...but I'm not sure if they are planning for their "one wild and precious life" as Mary Oliver would say! Here's the kicker—happy, healthy, and productive teachers foster happy, healthy, and productive students! It is critical that our "plans" include what is best for *everybody* in the magic show, and that means teachers taking care of teachers (a.k.a. self-care).

As teachers, we use lesson plans every day. But I have always dreamed of an addendum to our lesson plans referred to as "life plans." Teachers are barely finding time to create engaging, aligned, and differentiated lesson plans daily, so expecting them to plan for their own needs as well seems comical at best!

I see "life plans" as an answer to Maslow's Hierarchy of Needs. To be quite frank, I don't think we are fitting the bill. Here's a little sample of the application of Maslow's theory to teacher life. Let's start with physiological needs—I'm talking basics like water and air. Best of luck if you think you are going to regularly get a good night's sleep in this profession or show up to work in a cute outfit that's been washed or ironed. Let's just start with a "breathe in through your nose and out through your mouth!" Follow this up with at least five sips of water a day.

Moving on to safety needs. This could be everything from your health to your employment to your personal security at work. A first-year teacher at my school had a third-grade student threaten to bring a gun to school and shoot her. I'm betting she wasn't feeling in her safety zone that day. And she deserves a bonus check for showing up to work the next day following that unexpected outburst. Feeling safe is a very real need, and schools must examine the ways in which we assure that is happening for our educators.

Love and belonging? *You mean something other than the happy hour we would all like to be invited to? Isn't "margarita" a synonym for "love"? Your school family loves you!* All jokes aside, love and belonging means you have a right as an educator to spend meaningful, fun time with your friends and family. This includes a spouse and children of your own, if you so desire.

Let's continue our study of human motivation. Ready for esteem? Respect? Recognition, strength, and freedom? Please, my teacher friends, stop all of that giggling because I was just about to get to the top of the pyramid with self-actualization when you finally become the "most that you want to be!" Why are you falling on the ground? What do you mean your cheeks hurt from laughing? Can you please take my book seriously?

Okay, I feel the need to extend an author's apology for the sudden sarcastic tone. The irony is that I cannot stand sarcasm. I think this is indicative of the sheer frustration that I, along with most of my teacher sisters and brothers, feel regarding the availability and usage of our precious life—the time that we have on this planet.

Which brings us back to the **S.O.S.** (morse code: 3 dits, 3 dats, and another 3 dits). For years I have been consumed with the idea of "saving our teachers." In my work as an Instructional Mentor, we had all too many conversations about the importance of both recruiting and retaining excellent educators. *How do we keep, keep, keep, K-E-E-P this show going?*

But in the course of writing this book, I did a lot of reflection and came to the realization: *Hey, wait a minute! Wait just one little minute! It is not about anybody saving teachers.*

For Pete's Sake, who am I to steal your autonomy and agency right from under your feet? The S.O.S. needs to stand for "**S**aving **O**ur **S**elves!" *We* are the ones who must take charge of our own cups and start filling them up to the top and beyond to overflowing, Godspeed.

I spent years of my life working overtime in the classroom, and it left very little time for me to work on my own "life plan." However, I am one of the luckiest individuals to walk this earth when it comes to friendships. I have surrounded myself with other women who have encouraged (or should I say kidnapped) me to play, to set boundaries, and to find time for non-school related topics. Thank God for them.

I didn't have my first child until I was thirty-five. I was lost for almost twenty years in caring for my father, who had early onset Alzheimer's disease, and my mother, who fell ill after his passing. I was on a never-ending hamster wheel that kept spinning toward more life events that left me feeling unbalanced. It wasn't until I was 42 years old, when my father passed away, that I had this incredible surge of fearlessness. They say that happens sometimes in the face of death. His parting gift to me was the realization that *this is my life!* My one, great, big, beautiful life.

Thereafter, I started taking more chances and decided to

leave the classroom to become an Instructional Mentor. When they asked why I wanted the job, I replied, "When you get old enough to start plucking hairs from your chin, it is time to start coaching the next generation of teachers." I got the job, and I leveled up that year. It was the first time I could remember learning to be comfortable with discomfort. It was a turning point for me to truly realize that I must become the living, breathing model of what I was preaching. So, I went shopping for metaphorical oxygen masks and water: gift cards for fun places and a calendar to proactively schedule my time. For ME.

Are you in? Do you get it? If the plane is going down, the oxygen mask MUST go on your face first.

Listen up, my friends: the plane is going down. But there is always a good pilot that can bring it up again. Before fleeing to the exits, get that mask on and let's talk **S.O.S.** care. Teacher talk: a little of "this," a little of "that," and a little bit more of "this."

> *I was on a never-ending hamster wheel that kept spinning toward more life events that left me feeling unbalanced. It wasn't until I was 42 years old, when my father passed away, that I had this incredible surge of fearlessness. They say that happens sometimes in the face of death.*

~

Beyond your lesson plans, how are you managing your "life plans"?

- After the instructional plans are all laid out, what plans are you making for your one wild, precious life? Have you considered the importance of hitting all the rungs on the life ladder? In other words: physiological needs? Safety needs? Love and belonging? Esteem? Self-Actualization? You deserve to feel the peaceful balance that comes from living in a needs-fulfilling environment.
- Consider the positive impacts that meeting your personal needs can have on your students' academic and social and emotional well-being. What might be negative impacts of you **not** meeting these needs for yourself? (Not just effects on you, but on your students too?)

How does this impact the educator you are now?

- What happens when you are consistently placing a priority on self-care?
- What happens when you neglect your own self-care?
- How might you find a balance between work and home responsibilities and leisure activities?

Take-Away Time

- No matter how amazing, awesome, and wonderful you are—and I am guessing that is true about you or you wouldn't be reading this book!—if you fail to

plan for your own well-being, you will fall into the burnout trap.
- Knowledge of a hierarchy of needs is only helpful if you apply your learning to real life. Knowing is the simple part. Putting it into action is the hard part. That is the part that requires planning, purpose, and participation of other friends, family, and colleagues willing to support your efforts.
- Your well-being must come first! Oxygen mask on you…then on your students. By taking good care of yourself, you will avoid compassion fatigue, illness, resentment, and a whole other host of goodies that result from neglecting yourself.
- If you are feeling resentful or sarcastic, look at your own boundaries. Are you setting them at all? Truth: sometimes we get mad when we notice other people doing the things that we wish we were doing. Ugh.

Mindful Moment

- At the end of each day, gently rub your hands together. Imagine you are washing them clean and shaking away all the water, the germs, the remnants of the day. Use this as a closing moment as you focus on defining a clear line that exists between the end of a workday and the beginning of a "real life" afternoon and evening with yourself, your friends, your family, or all the above.

Ritual Reinforcement

- Consider rituals that could boost your mood on the way to or from work. Could you make a fun or relaxing playlist? Maybe you could listen to podcasts or motivational speeches on your commute. Perhaps you could call a buddy who helps you plan and problem-solve for the upcoming workday, or de-escalate or debrief as you drive home.
- Before you enter your home, breathe in through your nose and out through your mouth. Leave work outside of your home, so that you can be fully present in your life after work hours.

Daily Ritual Reading

- Self-care can be enhanced through the practice of gratitude. Have you started a gratitude journal yet? While I am fond of the saying, "Attitude of Gratitude" (I love me a good rhyme!) the reality is that genuinely feeling grateful takes a lot more than just *thinking* about it. Gratitude is a *practice*. This means the more you practice it, the easier it becomes to feel grateful on a daily basis. Each afternoon, write down 2-3 things for which you are grateful. End your workday on that note, not the one thing you think didn't go well. Your ritual reading for this can be your very own work!! Way to go...you are an author now, too.

Chapter 4

Balancing Your Account

Givers have to set limits because takers rarely do.

— Irma Kurtz

This giving thing we teachers do so well...does it have anything to do with the whole "infinity and beyond" deal? After all, it certainly appears as if we just keep giving and giving and giving with no end, like an emotional equivalent of the Energizer Bunny. Although I'm not sure if a battery charger is anywhere within sight for those of us who struggle to set healthy boundaries and limits. Unfortunately, the result can be resentful teachers who are angry at the unlimited expectations placed upon our profession.

We are teachers, that is true, but we could also match any

quick-change artist any day of the week as we throw our different hats into the air at the speed of light—therapist, mother, friend, collaborator, colleague, supporter, encourager, problem-solver, technology specialist, curriculum writer, assessor, trainer. I'm betting if I asked you to set a timer for two minutes and write down all your roles, the list would be longer than this page.

Our talents are to be commended, surely, but what do we do with those yucky feelings that creep up? The feelings of resentment, anger, frustration, and irritation that we just might like to blame on others instead of first looking at the "man in the mirror." As Michael Jackson lyricized, "He's asking you to change your ways!"

My dad was a tricky one, I say. Gosh dern, he would make me add "ing" to everything that was remotely negative. Let's practice: instead of "I am angry" it would become: "I am angering." Instead of "depressed," I am "depressing." Clearly, this didn't fit with all the words I used to express my feelings or the valid emotions that I was experiencing, but I think my tricky-but-wise dad was trying to make an important point. He wanted me to take some responsibility for what was going on in my world. I had a bad habit of always being the "giver." When imbalance kicked in, I began to realize I was the one sitting at the bottom of the seesaw, pushing my legs as hard as I could. Learning that it takes two to create a healthy balance was a valuable life lesson. I needed to pass some of the control over to the people sitting on the other side of the see-saw.

The whole "overdoing it" action was one I began to perfect as a child. By the time I began teaching, it was second nature to me to completely lose myself in work. Yes. *My name is Greta, and I am a workaholic!* Oh, here I go dipping back into my teacher story again. Remember those horrific photographs my mom showed me of my brother's accident? Well, it turns out that Princess Diana died in a pretty brutal car accident right around the ten-year anniversary of my brother's death. When the news started posting non-stop coverage of the mangled car, I began having bad dreams about my brother. For the first time in my life, I realized I needed somebody outside of my peer group and family to help me begin to process my loss. Time for a therapist. But here's the deal—I loved being in control. I was in so much control that I had compartmentalized all the grief that I should have expressed into a nice little box and tightly slammed the lid shut.

Now, the reason I was a control freak was a direct result of me not wanting to feel the terrible *out-of-control* feeling that I had after the accident. The pain of losing my brother—and, as I felt at the time, my mother as well—was excruciating. Being able to shine at work, to control my output in that setting, gave me a sense of peace. It was a good feeling. I was the Council for Exceptional Children's Rookie Teacher of the Year my first year, followed by multiple other "teacher of the year" accolades. Guys. I am not bragging. I am telling you straight-out that I had a *problem*. I was lost in a game of giving too much all the time to anybody who was wise enough to hang out with me for more than five seconds and realize that I was the girl to ask for a favor. The "buzz" came from being a giver and a hard worker and that felt really, really awesome to me. Like a drug. In fact, it was accompanied by a feeling of safety. I knew the expected outcomes of my hard work, which was the direct opposite of the unexpected and often erratic emotional responses generated by my grieving family at that time.

Unfortunately, anything in extreme can become unhealthy and lead to feelings of imbalance. And that is the lesson in this chapter. *Givers have to set limits*. We must find the healthy balance of both giving AND receiving.

Here's a little secret. Lean in for this one. *Other people like to "give" just as much as you do.*

Okay. Secret number two. *If you continue to give all the time without refilling your cup, your cup will be super, duper empty.*

Drumroll please.

"You cannot pour from an empty cup!" I believe the author of this statement is unknown. My God, where is this brilliant man or woman? And can you please be added to my best friend list immediately? Please bring lots of cups to our first playdate.

The wisest of educators must evolve to the point of realizing that the best mode of survival in this profession is to find your people—or better yet, strategically place yourself in the universe for them to find you. Okay, let's do both for higher chances of being sighted by the rescue crew. For me, that's how my greatest support started as a year-one teacher. I have never been afraid to ask questions and when I did find myself drowning right out of the gate, I had heard about a place called FDLRS (Florida Diagnostic and Learning Resources System). And that is where I met Doris.

I remember walking into the dusty old FDLRS building,

wondering, *Is there anybody in here that can help me? Anybody? Anybody?*

When I first glimpsed Doris, I believe there was light surrounding her and angelic harp music playing in the background. And then she floated toward me, lifted me up, and has never stopped doing so since that very first instant I laid eyes upon my own personal saint. She would become my second mother, role model, mentor, and therapist. She was the reason I survived my first year as an educator and she became the model of excellence by which I have lived my entire professional career. I would go on to surround myself with an unlimited number of brilliant mentors in the form of supervisors, instructional coaches, student services teams, trainers, and more. All willing to pour from their cups into mine.

Get your highlighters out, my teacher friends. I'm not a math whiz. In fact, I'm not entirely fond of math at all, but here's the deal. You must deposit into your account in order to withdraw. Overdrawn accounts incur additional charges that are no fun to pay. Balanced accounts begin to earn interest. That is good. Balanced accounts mean you have what you need to take care of yourself. When you take care of yourself, you can continue to happily take care of others. Balance your account.

> *Now, the reason I was a control freak was a direct result of me not wanting to feel the terrible out-of-control feeling that I had after the accident.*

∼

Check your statement?

- Imagine your life as a circle. Now, take a pencil and divide the circle into quadrants. Let's say: 1) physiological needs; 2) love and belonging; 3) work and productivity; and 4) family, friends, and fun. Quickly jot down all the things that fit into those categories. Now, stare at the circle. What do you see? Is it balanced, or do you find yourself looking at some areas that are more filled-up than others?
- How might you begin to take purposeful action to balance your circle? What activities, people, and places might you intentionally insert and where?

How does this impact the educator you are now?

- Thumbs-up if your cup is full. Thumbs-down if it is bone dry. To the side if you're doing "okay," but you can do better.
- How does "full-cup you" positively impact learning in your classroom?
- List ideas for "empty-cup you" to do starting right now to make changes for the better.

Take-Away Time

- Finding true balance in life is not an easy task. It can take a lifetime to examine the motivation and forces that drive our decision-making.

- Being vulnerable enough to look at yourself in the mirror and to take responsibility for your own actions can be a first step in setting healthy boundaries. Try that "ing" thing that my tricky dad used.
- Education is a field that will naturally suck the life out of you, if you let it. Oh. I know that sounds kind of dark, but it's really not. Let's flip the script. Educators who are balanced not only make a lasting impression on the lives of others, but they also claim a balanced and meaningful life for themselves that involves taking care of their personal needs, hobbies and interests, time with friends and family, and abundant love for self and others.

Mindful Moment

- Close your eyes and imagine that you are holding a warm cup of tea in your hand. (Or whatever your favorite drink might be.) Repeat after me: *My cup is full. I am an amazing giver, and my love flows over the rim of my cup. Let me share my gifts abundantly, so that others might drink from my talents for teaching and loving. Let it begin with me. Let me continuously pour into myself so that I might have more to share with others. I am worth it. In giving to myself, I am empowered to share with others the "interest" that I am earning in my account.*

Ritual Reinforcement

- Create a list of "deposits" and "withdrawals" for yourself. Imagine the people, places, and activities that fill you up, versus those that leave you feeling depleted. Add to your daily rituals by completing your deposit slips. Make sure you are entering these regularly.

Daily Ritual Reading

- Who is your self-care go-to author? Start researching now. I'm still loving Oprah and Brené Brown.
- Find your people and let their words be the cream and sugar in your cup.

Chapter 5

Harness Your Everyday Powers

Every adversity, every failure, every heartache carries with it the seed of an equal or greater benefit.

— Napoleon Hill

I'm a mama to two daughters. Of all the things I have accomplished in my lifetime, there are only two things that I truly want to get "right": Julia and Jaclyn. Every thought, every action, every feeling leads back to them. I have spent a lifetime giving of myself to other women's children, at times at my own daughters' expense, and for this I will spend the rest of my life praying to be the best mother I can be for them.

Having a teacher for a mom means you grow up in a classroom playing teacher yourself. It means you sit around for long afternoons waiting for your mother to finish lesson plans, grade tests, meet with parents. It means your mom often has to attend night-time functions and never stops talking about her job. Because teachers **never** stop talking about their jobs.

My daughters have watched me teach their entire lives. They have watched me lose myself in caretaking for both of my parents. They have watched me stand up for causes. They have watched me love myself and beat myself up. They have watched me sing and dance and joyfully experience all that life has to offer, and they have watched me ball up on the couch wondering what in the world I am going to do for my "next move." Like all mothers, there have been countless times when I have questioned my ability to parent, but as I watch my daughters grow into their twenties, I find myself entering a different phase. I find myself standing back and just admiring the women they are becoming. Both true masterpieces in progress. I am so grateful for my creations.

My daughters may not go into the field of education, but they are natural teachers. They respect the rights, hearts, minds, choices, and natural development of children as a direct result of living with me, a teacher, and their father, a former administrator. We are all so perfectly imperfect. Each one of us is more aware everyday of our own personal gifts. Each day, we are a little more accepting of the parts of us that might be rougher around the edges. We could be the poster family for: *We don't have it all figured out, but we do pretty amazing things!* We are currently working on an imaginary doctorate in the field of Normalizing All Feelings And Experiences.

I think I have finally figured out how to embrace the opportunities that come as a result of the challenges. I have enough "faith stories" at this point to see me through to the other side.

I worry at times that for years they have seen one of the primary forms of my identity present itself as a "caretaker". This word could be used to describe me in so many countless scenarios. They watched me take care of my father who had early onset Alzheimer's followed by years of caretaking for my mother after he passed away. They have seen me rush to the side of friends and colleagues experiencing divorce, financial woes, dissatisfaction with career choices, substance abuse. You name it, and Greta will rush to your side to listen and lead. Some might say she even has superpowers.

What I began to realize, though, is that it really isn't the superpowers that solve the world's problems—it's the everyday powers. It's the "put one foot in front of the other" actions that really change this world for the better. In fact, I needed to slow down (as fast as I could) to stop sending the message to my little women in the making that it is okay and healthy to jump into the fire with everybody all the time. Because, in fact, it is NOT. It's the surest path to burnout you can find, and I was at the head of the line screaming, "Look everyone. Over here! There's lots of trouble we can get into. Follow me!" Adhering only to this route led to my exhaustion and disappointment at times that I had no energy left after work to do the things I really enjoyed with my family. How much of that result did I need to own? How many personal choices had I made that led to my empty tanks? I wanted to cook, garden, sink my toes in the sand at the beach as we watched sunsets, read books, laugh, dance, and so much more. But it was more likely for you to find me snoozing away under my blankies by 7 p.m. because I was just too tired!

I'll never forget one night before my mother passed away. I had been working all day before I arrived at her home where my second job as her caregiver began. There were bills to pay, laundry to do, dishes to clean, food to cook, medicine to dispense. It took me until almost midnight to take care of all of these tasks, and at the end of the night I found myself staring into space, tears running down my cheeks. How much longer could I go on like this before I learned to reach out to others for help? How could I learn to take smaller steps at a more consistent pace to save myself from running out of fuel completely? My strength had been caring for others but it was becoming the very thing I hated the most about myself.

I want to clarify the importance of leaning into your strength and your passion. I loved being a helper and it made my heart extremely happy. However, learning that overdoing it to the extreme can lead to the unhealthy version of myself (tired, easily frustrated, disillusioned at times) was actually a big girl, super cool "aha" moment for me. We must study ourselves to become masters. Staring in the mirror at my own reflection gave me a moment to see who I truly wanted to be, and that is a woman who cares deeply about others, but who also cares about herself in equal measure. What will you do to lean into your strengths while maintaining the beauty of your own self-love?

Staring in the mirror at my own reflection gave me a moment to see who I truly wanted to be, and that is a woman who cares deeply about others, but who also cares about herself in equal measure.

How far would you go?
- How far will you allow yourself to go into the depths of exhaustion before you place yourself upon your care list? Doesn't our job literally feel like triage at times? I work in a transformation school, so on top of academic needs, I find myself assisting with behavioral support, mental health issues, food insecurity, students who are houseless, and more. Surrounding myself with a team of helpers reminds me that many hands make light work, and it allows me to honor the "helper" in others while balancing my own outpouring of love.

Take-Away Time
- Life is hard. Work gets in the way. Caretaking consumes us when our children are young and growing, or when our parents and family members age or become ill. Our loved ones will experience discomfort and challenge in the form of financial worries, divorce, etc. Even "fun" things can lead to us feeling depleted at times. Struggling to find balance in it all can leave us feeling empty or "less than."
- It's okay. It's all okay. Life isn't supposed to be peachy every day. It's tangled and messy. Beautiful and bouncy. Straight-up and curvy. Normalize the variance in emotion and experience. Give your children and onlookers permission to see the good, the bad, and every little thing in between! Let them see how you beautifully navigate it all.
- At some point in life, you will harness a superpower that you never knew you had inside of you, in order to overcome a

big obstacle. Use it for good. The truth is that you will go into hyperdrive with your "everyday" powers. You already have what it takes to do this life thing! If you are feeling unsure of yourself at any time, reach out that hand when it needs lifting. Remember, your helpers are on call at all times!

Mindful Moment

Lie down and close your eyes. Get some meditation music going and begin to breathe in through your nose and out through your mouth. Repeat after me:

I am safe and I am loved. I have nothing to fear because I am wrapped in a protective bubble of love and warmth and security. I have everything that it takes to do this work, and nothing is stronger than my ability to handle this situation. It is okay if I need to step away and care for myself first in order to be stronger for others. I can break down big tasks into smaller steps without being judged.

Ritual Reinforcement

Keep a picture frame of your favorite friends and family on your desk. Remind yourself each day of why you continue to do hard things. Look at the faces who are ready to support you and ask for help when you need it.

Daily Reading

Think of the statements, readings, or song lyrics that comfort you and find time everyday to absorb them. One of my favorites is from St. Francis of Assisi:

> *"Lord, make me an instrument of your peace: where there is hatred, let me sow love; where there is injury, pardon; where*

there is doubt, faith; where there is despair, hope; where there is darkness, light; where there is sadness, joy."

Chapter 6

Spaces and Places

Beautiful places are almost alive! When you visit them, you can feel their breaths!

— Mehmet Murat Ildan

The mentor, teacher, coach, and leader in me would love to take a moment for a good recap. We've hopefully made some worthwhile discoveries in chapters one through five. Perhaps you:

- Have a clearer picture of your own teacher story. Knowing your "why" for anything enhances your purpose and your output. It guides you into the future, while also rooting you to solid ground.

- You might appreciate my little idea of gathering "faith stories." If you would like to get a good grade in this class, please purchase a journal and start collecting your full-circle moments. Your life is full of vignettes with you as the main character overcoming great challenges with grace, dignity, respect, and newfound brilliance! This treasure trove of evidence can see you through difficult scenarios in the future, as they help remind you of your inner strength.
- As teachers, lesson planning is critical to the success of our days, weeks, months, and school years. It is always happening and continuously changing based on your most recent assessments, observations, reflections, and "aha!" moments related to what is in the best interest of students. Are you taking the time to do the same thing for yourself? Don't forget my idea about the addendum at the end of your school plans called "life plans"— a little of "this," a little of "that," and a little bit more of "this." Your life plan should literally begin with self-care related to your most basic needs such as water, sleep, and healthy foods, including time for yourself, your friends and family, and activities that enrich your own existence. There is a huge difference between *knowing* this is good for you and doing it. Please, start DOING IT!
- Chapter 4: Balancing Your Account. This seems to be the one that still likes to hit me over the head

with a great, big, ol' hammer. In a profession that revolves around giving, it is imperative that you keep your account balanced at all times. Otherwise, you risk losing your greatest gift—that of helping others—to ultimate resentment, anger, and frustration. It is easy to get lost trying to figure out how to meet your own needs. Fill your cup. Fill it with something that is delicious to drink!! Find your support people and allow yourself to be nurtured and strengthened by their gifts as well as your own. Continue to be a great giver, but dabble in accepting the love and wisdom of others.

- Slow down and harness your everyday powers to take super action in your life. Let *your* helpers become involved in your self-care as your assistants and accountability partners.

This brings us to chapter six. We've done some "inner" work, but what I have always personally experienced as an educator is that, in order for the ultimate journey of true learning to take place, my "outside" must also be a place of great peace for me and my students.

I have spent years creating inviting spaces in the classroom for my students because I have seen the connections this generates inside their growing brains. For fun, you can check out my Facebook page at S.O.S.: *Survival Guide for Teachers Old and New* to see some photos of my special spaces and places, in hopes of inspiring you to create yours.

One of my favorite eras in my career was teaching first grade for seven years alongside the most amazing team of women. They were and always will be my "dream team." We worked hard, but we played hard too, and a big part of that was creating inviting corners for children to discover the wonder of learning!

One year, we read by imaginary campfires made of rolled-up brown bags and fiery red tissue paper as we sat on oversized stuffed horses! Another year, I transformed my entire classroom into a French café where we devoured baguettes and sipped lemonade while speaking in French accents all day! *Ooooh la la,* was that fun!

The last seven years of my life have been devoted to social and emotional learning, restorative practices, behavioral support, and mindfulness. Those are my favorite spaces to create—the ones that elevate, relax, de-escalate, promote peace, foster self-awareness, strengthen relationships, and allow for children and adults to feel safe and valued.

In my current room, I have clearly designated spaces for all these activities. My favorite spot is my peace table. The letters P-E-A-C-E grace the surface where we gather, along with our agreements for how we speak and listen from our hearts. The lights are low and soft music flows in the background. There I lead a generation of young thinkers down a path of restoration that encourages them to hear and honor the stories of others. They have time and space to speak their own truths, and to imagine what healing might look like so that all perspectives can be respected and contribute to an anthology of personal growth.

- And finally, at home, I have my "teacher treasure" drawer. It is overflowing with notes and cards of love and affirmation that go back to my very first year of teaching. I reread them when I need to remember my "why." I'll never forget a little girl in my class my very first year of teaching, whose father passed away on Halloween. She came to school in clown make-up and fully costumed, sobbing. Her mother did not want her to go to the funeral, so I offered for her to stay with me outside of school instead. I still have the card expressing gratitude from her mother, and I will never regret being able to share that day with her at such an impactful moment in her young life. She knew that day that she was loved and valued in my safe space. The smallest act of spending time with a hurting child in a safe place can make an impression that lasts a lifetime. I read that note repeatedly to remind myself of this.

Gather your goodies and create your own "treasure box" so that you might delight in this same practice. Trust me, it will feed your teacher soul.

She knew that day that she was loved and valued in my safe space.

What do your spaces and places look like?

- Look around your classroom. What feelings immediately arise? Do you feel peaceful or cluttered? Organized or disorganized? Clear on your path for learning, or wondering where each activity and lesson should take place?
- Is your room arranged to support the following:
- Whole group time
- Small group time
- Independent time
- A "meeting" place for special occasions like read-alouds, social and emotional learning, or restorative practices
- A classroom library or place to access math, science, social studies, or writing materials
- A place to keep backpacks and/or cell phones
- An area to display student data or outstanding work samples
- Space for anchor charts or visuals to enhance student learning, such as "word walls"
- Easy access to classroom supplies
- Desk arrangement to support collaborative discussions among students
- A safe place or a reflection spot
- If you are feeling overwhelmed, imagine small steps that you could take to bring a greater sense of order to things. Prioritize your next moves. Could clearing off your desk or group table be step number one?

Take-Away Time

- Our work to S.O.S. or **S**ave **O**ur **S**elves must begin on the inside and work its way out. With that being said, the spaces and places we create in our classrooms and our homes can be arranged to support our peace and our planning efforts.
- Taking the time to create organized and peaceful places can support the delivery of more effective instruction, procedures, and routines within the classroom. Mindfulness, social and emotional competence, self-reflection, and restoration benefit as well.
- Little acts of creativity can enhance learning and the culture of your classroom—like campfires and French cafes! These special places you create are the backdrop for the magic show.
- Having one special spot such as a "teacher treasure drawer" houses the power of words we all need at times to remember our "why," or to enjoy words of appreciation and affirmation for our hard work.

Mindful Moment

- Find music that resonates with you. It might be meditation music. It might be smooth jazz, dancing music, music that makes you cry in a good way, or some hard rock! Get those musical notes flowing as you take a moment to really *notice* what is in your classroom. Look around and notice what you see. What you hear. What you smell. Connect with the spaces that bring you the most joy or motivation. Imagine improving the ones that don't serve you, so that when you and your students are at work, you feel invited into a wonderland of great discovery with your learning.

Ritual Reinforcement

- I always say that my college job at Häagen-Dazs prepared me for teaching and motherhood. If there was time to lean, there was time to clean! And the very distinct opening and closing procedures defined clear lines for me as an employee for the beginning and ending of each shift. What could you do within your spaces and places to bring that same ritual of clear lines? How could you begin and end each day with routines that support your spaces and places?

Daily Ritual Reading

- Looking for ideas for beautiful spaces? Try doing a search on the internet and get lost in the "too many to count" possibilities that include anything from nature to sensory spaces to ultimate classroom settings that we can only dream about. Writing grants and reaching out to local churches and community partnerships is a great way to fund your dreams. That's what I've done, and I have found a million helpers in the world who believe in the same dreams I do. Thank you, Ms. Brittany from Bay Hope Church for sharing in my vision for my Mindful Mustangs room!

Chapter 7

Road to Resilience

With everything that has happened to you, you can either feel sorry for yourself or treat what has happened as a gift. Everything is either an opportunity to grow or an obstacle to keep you from growing. You get to choose.

— Wayne Dyer

Cultivating strong teachers and students, sturdy grown-ups, and courageous children, takes the green thumb of a master gardener, indeed. We must also take notice to masterfully place our seeds in just the right soil, sunlight, water, and composition of nutrients to reap the harvest. It is not enough in the field of education to bounce back from the day-to-day challenges, shifts, and demands, but rather we must develop a talent for moving forward in a trajectory of continuous growth. If we are meant to thrive in this profession, it most assuredly helps if our work is done with a happy heart.

As an avid reader and language-lover, I catch myself wondering and wondering all the time. In my work as a reading teacher, I would remind my students that good readers ask questions 24/7! (More math. Yikes. Pretty easy-peezy though. This one just means: ALL THE TIME!) And it is so true. What I probably love most about learning is that it is a constant cycle of inquiry. So fascinating. The minute I learn one thing, I am wondrously connecting it to something else I want to know more about, as well.

Back to the "ooohs" and "ahhhs" of the magic show, peeps! And what makes a good educator a magician is that they effortlessly intertwine all this information with classroom procedures and management plans, relationship and culture-building, lesson plan and delivery, assessment and analysis, home-school communication, and more! Pay close attention, audience, because the best ones make it appear as if they are doing nothing, that's how good they are.

What must be considered, though, is that educators are giving of themselves constantly, and the majority of America is asking them to reach into their pockets and try to find even more to give. For free. My mother used to always tell me, "Please don't try to figure out your hourly rate, because you won't like the answer!" She beamed with pride for the contribution I made to the world daily, while worrying sick about the lack of balance I had between that giving-and-receiving thing I mentioned in chapter four. Mama was right though. To truly serve my students in the deep and nurturing way in which my beloved Raggedy Ann doll was accustomed, I needed to develop and—even more importantly, **utilize**—resiliency strategies for enduring the long haul.

My mentor told me stories of when she first began teaching, how her teacher "mothers" took her under their wing and would even help her plan out what she was going to eat for dinner! She, in turn, mentored me as if I were her own daughter, and to this day she contributes to the livelihood of my entire family. Connections between teachers run deep. My teacher sisters could call me at 3 a.m. and my only question if they needed me would be, "Do I put a bra on first or just run? Cuz' I'm coming, girl!"

My worry for our newest generation of teachers is that their veteran cohorts are tired in a way that gives a whole new meaning to the word. We are struggling financially, we float down tributaries that have led us away from our own self-care, many of us are tied up in caring for aging and dying parents, and don't get me started on the aftermath of COVID or the ramifications of a country divided by politics. Can't we all just get along? I vote for sandboxes across the country and mandatory "Be a good friend" training.

It is my hope with this book, that teachers (and all of us who love our teachers) take note that we must all work together to support their survival. We cannot walk this planet without them. Or at least not in the way that matches our hopes and visions for the future. In my dreams, my daughters will be accepting and loving others with a greater capacity than ever imagined. They will be serving the world in professions that don't even exist now, that little humans are only dreaming about as we speak. And it will be a teacher that ignites a flame so fierce in that child that *it shall and will be done!*

How can we do this? Well, I've only begun to touch the surface in this book—my sketches of a survival guide for my old friends and for the new teachers breathing a fresh perspective on what learning could and should look like now and in the future. I know that research doesn't necessarily support homework, but I'm going to assign some anyway, okay? Because what I do know is that anything truly worth having demands effort. My best learning has come when I allow myself to accept discomfort as a part of the journey. I have been given a gift for finding the best in situations. My obstacles, tears, and challenges have truly been invitations to grow into the best version of myself.

And so, your homework is to deeply reflect upon the following questions:

> *It is not enough in the field of education to bounce back from the day-to-day challenges, shifts, and demands, but rather we must develop a talent for moving forward in a trajectory of continuous growth.*

What questions do I need to ask?

- How can I continue to develop and understand my own teacher story—all the smooth and shiny

layers, but the crusty ones as well? How might I add daily reflection as a tool for identifying my strengths and areas on which I can continue to build strong foundations for myself and my learners?
- What is the best way to unleash a growth mindset that serves me in a way that opens my vision to see situations as *opportunities,* as opposed to crises that are mountains too tall to climb?
- Who do I turn to for the reminder that change is part of life? What will continually remind me that I have roots strong enough to bend, but flexible enough to sway with the wind, guiding me in directions that will lead me to better days.
- How do I prioritize actions worth taking, while also matching it with the energy necessary to make things happen?
- What resources are available to me to nurture self-discovery, self-care, and self-love?
- How can I reinforce activities that bring me hope and balance, so that my battery can recharge on a regular basis?

Take-Away Time

- Teachers are superhumans. Born to the world to make it better. Created to create all other professions. Walking this earth to keep it spinning.
- We are *all* teachers in some sense.

- There are many valid experiences and feelings that contribute to teacher burn-out and overwhelm, but we also have the skill level to reflect, assess, and take charge of our futures, so that we can counter those flames.
- Knowing where you come from will help guide you in the direction of your wild and precious future.
- Where there is pain, there is growth. Where there is a challenge, there is opportunity. Where there is belief, there is positive impact.
- Find your village. Your team. Your people. Your gardeners. Your helpers. Your cheerleaders. The people who applaud you from the balcony. Hold them near the softest part of your heart and the highest part of your brain.

Mindful Moment

- Take a moment. You can play some nice meditation music or just sit quietly in peaceful silence. You can keep your eyes open, lower your gaze, or shut your eyes. You. You, my dear reader, are the one who oversees you. It is *you* who must save yourself. Breathe in through your nose and out through your mouth, and celebrate this magical ride you have chosen to take.

Let a soft blue light enter that amazing head of yours. Imagine it washing through your magnificent brain, peacefully clearing out any files that are getting in the way of the life-changing work you do. Let the light continue to travel down to your mouth that thinks before it speaks every day; that intentionally and purposefully orchestrates the power of word exchange with others. See that light traveling down into your throat, alleviating your worries that are trying to manifest themselves into expressions. And now, that soft blue light is running toward that big heart of yours that can barely fit inside of your chest because it is so full of love. This light is now traveling abundantly through your arms and hands, your legs, and feet—the parts of your body that enable you to move into action daily as you give so freely to others.

Give thanks for your body. Give thanks for the gifts that you have been given to hold the highest and most important profession—that of an educator.

I see you. I hear you. I notice you. I value you. Repeat after me: I am seen. I am heard. I am noticed. I am valued. Sit quietly for as long or as little as you need to allow yourself to believe that you *are* the magic show.

Ritual Reinforcement

- Allow yourself 5 minutes a day to read positive affirmations. Find some that you like and create some of your own. Here are a few examples that might specifically apply to teachers:
- I work hard to make the lives of my students more fulfilling. I, too, deserve to have my needs met. Today, I will prioritize my own needs first, so that I can be a better giver.

- I am resilient. I am capable of handling difficult situations because I am empowered with skills and talents that allow me to do so. I will use my toolbox today.
- I am tired today, and that is okay. When I pull back to recharge, it enables me to go full force tomorrow. My self-care matters.
- I have "everyday" powers for moving situations forward. I will stop, look, and listen, so that I can do this thing!

Daily Ritual Reading

- If you are looking for some inspiration, why not hop on a few TED Talks? Grab some self-help books. Google some inspirational poetry. Go back and reread the reflection sections of my book. The world is waiting to support you. Find your helpers.

Chapter 8

I'm So Glad We Had This Time Together

I'm so glad we had this time together just to have a laugh, or sing a song. Seems we just got started and before you know it comes the time we have to say, 'So long.'

— Joe Hamilton

When I was a little girl, probably just a couple of years after meeting Raggedy Ann and beginning my career as her teacher, my mother used to ask me what I wanted to be when I grew up.

I always replied with confidence and pure joy, "Carol Burnett!" Our family spent countless hours together laughing until we cried watching her comedic sketches and hilarious characters. She was perfect to me, and still is. So good, just so good at what she was born to do!

I still cry (happy tears) picturing her gentle ear tug used to communicate with her grandmother from the stage of each episode. I think of that loving gesture as a part of her brand, her image. Her recognition came from being a triple threat! She could sing, dance, and perform, while laughing her way through life's "bloopers" as well. She made me wonder what I want to be remembered for.

I would like to think that I have grown into what I was meant to do, and that is to be a teacher. I would be remiss if I did not use this last opportunity to thank Raggedy Ann for training me so well. Like my role model, Ms. Carol, I hope I am remembered as a "triple threat." My motto: "Laughing, learning, and lifting!" My students would tell you that in Woolley's Wonderland of Learning we have lots of fun, we love growing our brains and our hearts, and we lift each other up when things get tough.

What represents you and your image? Do you set high expectations? Build great relationships with students and families? Reach the *whole* child—mind, body, and spirit?

As I stated in my very first chapter, I would come to know details about my life that contributed to every part of who I was and why I was truly called to be an educator. A caretaker. A believer. An encourager. A trainer. A mentor. An understander of human behavior. The details unraveling like a thread being pulled from the hem of a ragged dress that just kept getting longer and longer. So, I will begin the end with this:

I am a teacher.
I was born to be a teacher.
I will always be a teacher.
I was meant to be a teacher.
I will live, breathe, and die being a teacher.
I am proud to be a teacher.
I will always elevate, support, and cry out for other teachers.
I will fight to save our teachers.
I will never give up on teachers.

I believe that teachers are the most important humans on the planet.

But what I also know now, is that it is going to take some self-work—some "**s**ave **o**ur **s**elves" work—to maintain the level of excellence deserved by every individual teacher and student that inhabits our world. That's all of us, guys. Because we are **all** students and teachers. All. Of. The. Time.

Won't you join me in my ***movement*** of empowerment? Your story matters to me. There is a destiny that made us brothers and sisters. Together, we can do this. A movement begins with one voice calling out to others to join the chorus. Won't you sing along with me?

> ...it is going to take some self-work—some "**s**ave **o**ur **s**elves" work—to maintain the level of excellence deserved by every individual teacher and student that inhabits our world.

Afterword
Meet Me In The Middle

There will come a time when you believe everything is finished. That will be the beginning.

— Louis L'Amour

I love this quote by Robert Frost:

"Ends and beginnings? There are no such things. There are only middles."

That is my wish for this book—that it becomes your fascinating new middle! I envision words of wisdom and encouragement cascading into the hearts and minds of individuals and small groups of educators open to receiving this message right now at this present moment in time. The place we will meet is somewhere in the center of what you already know and what you are craving to do in your life right now to unleash beautiful, unknown possibilities for yourself.

In this book, I have captured eight big ideas (The Great Eight) that can be utilized for book clubbing, workshopping, journaling, podcasting, and story writing. Stay tuned for more. This is only the beginning. You already know what to do, you just need to connect to the energy that will allow you to bring it to life. Find out more by following my *S.O.S.: Survival Guide for Teachers Old and New* Facebook Page. Here you will be able to connect with other like-minded educators to share your teacher and faith stories, check out pictures of what I am doing at school, receive mentoring for life plans that include personal and professional needs, find out about upcoming podcast episodes, and more! I can't wait to meet you there.

The Great Eight

- **USE YOUR NARRATIVE TO DEFINE YOUR PAST, PRESENT, AND FUTURE**: Develop a clear picture of your "why" for work and home and use this as a guide to maintaining your focus with your goal-setting and action plans.
- **FIND YOUR FAITH STORIES**: The stories that will remind you that you have what it takes to use challenges as opportunities for growth and develop a skill-set that empowers you to persevere through demanding professional and personal scenarios.
- **CREATE LIFE PLANS THAT MEET ALL OF YOUR NEEDS, *PERSONAL AND*

PROFESSIONAL: Ensure that you are creating a needs-fulfilling life that includes self-care and work-life balance; solidify a plan for accountability that includes frequent reflection on real strengths and areas for development.

- BALANCE YOUR GIVE-AND-TAKE: Define priorities and your locus of control; learn to identify the best places for you to offer your talents to others while becoming comfortable with delegation, collaboration, and equity of roles and responsibilities.
- HARNESS YOUR "EVERYDAY" POWERS: Zone in on your strengths and your individual personality style, and use it to maximize your happiness and productivity.
- SHAPE SPACES AND PLACES: Create clearly designated areas that support your personal and professional goals guided by peace, productivity, and intentionality.
- PAVE A ROAD TO RESILIENCE: Learn and utilize skills for resiliency that empower you to not just "bounce back" but move forward.
- BUZZ YOUR BRAND: Become confident with what makes you special, and decide for what you want to be known and remembered—make your mark!

Acknowledgments

To all the students, families, colleagues, and administrators with whom I have had the honor of working throughout my career, thank you. It is all of you who have been my true inspiration and helped me to write the best stories of my life.

To my writing coach extraordinaire, Dallas Woodburn, thank you for believing that there was a book growing inside of me and for nurturing it into reality. You have been one of my greatest teachers, and I will be eternally grateful for your guidance and talent. Most importantly, I am thankful for your oversized heart. Abundant gratitude also goes out to her amazing team of "book elves." I never knew the endless love and hours that actually go into placing a book upon a shelf. Thank you to my book interior designer Staci Olsen, my cover designer Katarina, and publishing wiz Karen Delano. You rock!

To Doris Renick, my "Giving Tree," thank you for being the mentor and mother of my dreams. It is you who taught me how to live with gratitude and grace.

To all my dear friends who were willing to read my baby book and provide me with honest feedback and reflection, so that I might continue to grow. Thank you for taking your precious time to do that and for helping me to be vulnerable in this process of learning how to write a book.

To Aimee Ballans, thank you for the gifts you gave me during all our mentor training academies, and for writing the introduction. You are the best listener I have ever met, and your ability to grow others into the best version of themselves blows me away.

Finally, to my amazing family. To my brother and sister, my mom and dad, Chris, Julia, and Jaclyn. Thank you for making me feel seen, heard, and deeply loved. Thank you for proving daily that unconditional love harnesses a life-altering energy that changes the world for the better.

About the Author

Greta Woolley has happily been serving students, families, and teachers for over thirty years in both general and exceptional student education settings. She currently resides and works in Tampa, Florida in the Transformation Network, promoting strong connections between colleagues and learning communities. Her work as a teacher on the front lines, ESE Specialist, Instructional Mentor, District Trainer, and Site-Based Behavior Specialist has earned her many awards at a district, state, and national level.

She graduated from the University of Florida with both a bachelor's and a master's degree in Education with an emphasis in Special Education, including post-master work in Reality Therapy and Social and Emotional Learning.

This is Greta's first book, and she dreams of writing many more with a true desire to positively impact the most important profession she knows—that of a teacher.

When she is not walking beside educators and students, she can be found adoring her husband and two beautiful daughters, and probably giggling at the antics of a couple of dachshunds, surrounded by the joy of her garden.

Made in the USA
Columbia, SC
01 April 2025